Humor Around Horses

Stu Campbell

Illustrations by R. Loren Schmidt

ISBN: 978-0-9675164-2-4

Cover and text design by D.K. Luraas

Printed and bound in the United States of America

Contents

The Value of a Horse 1

Just How Good a Friend Are You? 7

The Obvious is Not so Obvious 11

Cuddles 13

Aromas 17

Turn-About's Fair Play 21

Language Barrier 25

The Right Horse for the Right Rider 29

The Cook 35

Memory Loss 39

Questions 43

Trying to Help? 47

Work Ethics 51

Is Right Wrong? 59

A Journeyman 65

Personality Conflicts 71

Hospitality 77

The Naturalist 81

Hoolihan 85

Hats 89

Training 93

Dick Bolton 99

A Surprise 103

No Sense of Humor 107

"A cowboy is a man with guts and a horse."
—Will James

"Cowgirls can do everything a cowboy can do—
they just look better doing it."
—Anonymous

"The outside of a horse is
good for the inside of a man."
—Winston Churchill or
Will Rogers or somebody

"I wish I had said that."
—Stu Campbell

The Value of a Horse

Trying to figure out how much a horse is worth can be a tough problem. I guess a horse is worth whatever a person pays for him. But when a feller starts a horse business, he's got to be real careful how much he spends on each particular animal.

Such was the problem I had in the spring of 1989. Pat Mantle had lent me $39,000.00 on a handshake to start my own rental horse stables. I had a good location and I thought I could start with about forty head of good dependable horses—I could build up a sizeable, useable herd of rental horses.

But I had a real problem—I couldn't find the horses I needed. I was hoping Pat could lease me a bunch, but all his horses were committed for the summer. Pat put me onto a guy, Dobbin, near Durango, Colorado, that might have some horses I could use, but Dobbin's horses were all committed.

I was beginning to think that this might be an exceptional year in the horse rental business and I would miss out on it because I didn't have any horses.

Dobbin put me onto Hal Koenig in Bayfield, Colorado.

Dobbin thought he might have some horses. I felt like we hit the jackpot when I called Hal and he said he could probably fill my order.

I took my oldest boy, Will, out of school and we made the trip to Bayfield. We had our saddles and were ready to try out some horses.

We ended up buying twenty-four horses from Hal, consisting of all kinds, colors, and sizes. On the way home, I was reflecting on what kind of people would work on each horse I bought when Will asked me, "What are you going to use that three-year-old you bought for?"

In this bunch of horses was a three-year-old thoroughbred colt that I figured we could use for a guide horse until he got some age to him and we could teach him some manners. Some of these dude horses aren't really too dependable until they get to be eight or nine years old.

I had hired a feller that previously worked for me at Sombrero Stables in Grand Lake named Jeff Bowling. Jeff was a pretty fair hand and I thought he could probably make a good horse out of the colt.

When Jeff showed up to work, I had him ride the colt but for some reason or other, Jeff didn't like him. I rode him later and found out he was kinda rough riding. He put his feet down like he was pounding nails in a cement sidewalk.

Jeff kept putting his saddle on another horse and Will kept saddling the colt. Finally, Will asked me if he could have the colt as his guide horse.

I let Will ride the as yet unnamed colt as I didn't have anybody else to ride him and didn't want to rent him out. But I did have some misgivings—Will had never trained a horse before. The horse had been started and all he needed was some further education.

Will rode the horse and did a good job with him, in fact he did such a good job that he didn't want to rent him out. He became Will's guide horse.

Will approached me one day and asked, "What would you sell Bill for?" He had named the horse after himself in a fashion.

This presented quite a problem for me. I'd paid five hundred dollars a head for the first twenty-four horses I bought from Hal. My formula for buying horses was pretty simple. At ten bucks for an hour's ride, with roughly one hundred days a season, if we used the horse one hour a day that would work out to a $1,000.00. If we used him for two hours half of those hundred days, that would work out to $1,500.00 income for the summer per horse.

I explained to Will that the horse really wasn't worth the $500.00 we gave for him, but we expected to make at least $1,500.00 on the horse. Then just for the fun of it, I added, "The horse really ain't worth nothin'. As a guide horse, he ain't made a cent."

"Then why don't you give him to me?" Will asked.

"We started this deal to make money, an' with all the horses we got, the bills we have to pay, I can't afford to be givin' away anything. If I was to sell any of these horses, I'd have to sell him for at least as much as I expected to make on him, or more. Besides that," I added, "You can't afford to buy him!" I knew how much I was paying Will for wages.

The boy left a little dejected, but continued to ride the horse. Actually, he had the horse pretty well trained; he would do about anything but come in the house to eat. I wouldn't allow that.

I came back from town one day, and Will come up to me and said, "You gotta sell Bill to me and you gotta sell him for ten bucks."

"How come," I says, somewhat amused.

"You said you would sell the horse for what he made during the summer. While you were gone, I rented him out for an hour. He's made ten bucks, so that's what he's worth! You gotta sell him to me for ten bucks."

The reasoning was fairly sound, but I couldn't go for the deal.

Just How Good a Friend Are You?

I work for my friend, Dave Weller, at Moraine Park Stables in Rocky Mountain National Park just outside Estes Park, Colorado. I've worked for Dave for a number of years, going back to the winter of 1986–87, when I managed South Mountain Stables in Phoenix, Arizona.

I've always admired Dave, particularly his horse knowledge and skills. He rides both English and Western and has a room full of ribbons and trophies to prove it. He's always had good horses to ride and they have the bloodlines to prove it. He's not afraid to spend a lot of money if he figures the horse is worth it, so he's got a good string of personal horses.

The rental horses he buys are pretty good horses, but he doesn't spend the money on them as he might when he's buying horses for himself.

Dave is pretty proud of his horses and I've never seen anyone ride them other than himself.

When we started the 2008 summer season we only had twenty-five head of horses. This was the fewest number of horses Dave had ever had to start a season, and he'd run the Moraine Park Stables for more than twenty years. This twenty-five head

Loren Schmidt

of horses that we had included guide horses, so we were really limited as to the number of riders we could take out at any one time. My own guide horse hadn't showed up, so I was riding some rental horses that could use some extra work before we rented them out.

It turned out that someone had signed up a group of riders with more people than we had horses for. We were looking to get more horses, but they wouldn't be in until after the big group had scheduled their ride. This caused a big problem for Dave and me—it's not good for a business to overbook their reservations. Dave and I spent a lot of time considering our options, without success. The person who took the reservation hadn't taken the phone number of the group leader, so we couldn't call and confirm the reservation or the number of people and make some other adjustments. It was really a tough situation.

The day for the ride was fast approaching and the situation was becoming more stressful every hour. Dave was down at the corral, trying to figure out what to do when he turned to me.

"Any suggestions," he asked.

"Nothing," I replied.

"Well," he said, "If worse comes to worse, you can ride my red dun horse."

I was flabbergasted! Using one of Dave's horses hadn't even occurred to me. At the same moment I was shocked and even somewhat honored. Dave was the only one that rode his horses!

Surprised, I said, "That's quite an honor, Dave! To what do I owe this favor, for which I'm sure I'll be in debt to you for the rest of my life? I've never seen anyone but you ride your horses."

I admit I was sorta looking forward to this proposition, but didn't really know how to take it. I actually thought there might even be a compliment in the works.

"That's no big deal," said Dave. "I was going to sell the horse this summer anyway."

The Obvious is Not so Obvious

Occasionally, people fall off horses. Most of the time they aren't hurt and everything is okay. At our horse rental stables, every time someone hits the ground whether there are any injuries or not, we have to fill out an incident report form for insurance purposes. This creates some extra paper work, but it has to be done.

We had a young lady, she was six or seven, fall off her horse one day. She was not hurt, but we had to fill out the required paperwork. Apparently, she got to leaning out of the saddle to look at a flower, and when she leaned far enough, gravity took effect and she hit the ground.

Her mother had sent the family on the ride and remained behind. As the ride approached the stable, there was the customary waving and greetings. The youngster's brothers and sisters were all laughing as they informed their mother that their sister had fallen off her horse.

The mother immediately became very concerned, almost distraught. Her youngest daughter had fallen off her horse and while there were no injuries—no cuts, abrasions, no bruises, no broken bones—the mother was almost hysterical.

I ushered the family and other members of the ride into the office to fill out the incident report form. As I passed out the forms, the mother could not keep from asking questions, like, "What happened?" and "How did it happen?" During this barrage of questions directed at the daughter, she didn't give the youngster an opportunity to even answer. Her most frequent question, as she felt the girl's arms and legs, checking for broken bones, was "Where did you land?"

Mom asked this question so much without giving the youngster a chance to answer, that even the young girl was becoming frustrated.

When Mom asked the question, "Where did you land?" one too many times, the girl, very frustrated, effectively silenced her mom by answering, "On the ground!"

I could surely appreciate the mother's concern, but I found a very high appreciation for the young lady as she very efficiently and effectively and promptly put an end to her mother's seemingly endless questioning!

Cuddles

I sure wouldn't have named him Cuddles. I didn't much care for the horse. He had too much energy and for a dude horse, that can have some adverse effects. I figured all that energy could be rode out of him, but it would take some time. He could also use some work on his neck reining and he could certainly use better ground manners.

I rode the horse a few times and decided he would be all right with a lot of work. However, I didn't ride him after the stable-hands, Mandy and Megan, named him Cuddles. I just couldn't really be comfortable with that name; to me it just didn't fit. I think the girls named him that just to get to me. They did. To me, the most redeeming feature of the horse was that he wasn't too tall. He was short, only about fourteen hands high, therefore easy to get on. This is very important to an old, stove-up cowboy like me.

His ground manners left a lot to be desired. He proved this one day when Dave was resetting a hind shoe. The horse pulled his foot before Dave had a chance to bend a nail over. This action by Cuddles almost cut Dave's finger off, and we had to take him to the hospital for some stitches.

Dave hadn't finished shoeing the horse and had left the nail unclenched. There was about three-quarters of an inch of the nail sticking straight up out of the hoof and three or four nails that still needed to be set. The shoeing job was not done!

I never figured myself to be an expert farrier, and there wasn't anyone else who could put on a shoe, so I had to finish the job.

It had been quite a few years since I had been involved in shoeing a horse and I knew my back wasn't in shape for this kind of work, but the job had to be finished. Besides, that nail sticking up had to be tended to. If Cuddles should roll, he could very well disembowel himself. Even if he kicked a fly off his stomach, the results could be disastrous. Nope, the job had to be done and I was the only one who could do it!

I had expected some trouble from Cuddles as I finished the shoeing job, but the horse stood pretty good for me as I clinched the nail and drove the others. I completed the job and dressed up the foot a little, but not much. I was tired and my back told me I was too old for this kind of work! I was reminded why I didn't take up horseshoeing as a career.

We had Travis, another stablehand, ride Cuddles and he actually liked the horse, name and all. Travis seemed to get along with the horse and was doing a lot of stuff on the trail with the horse that was not exactly appropriate, but sometimes it would help put the more nervous riders at ease. I kinda thought some of the stuff Travis was doing might get him into some trouble and suggested he not do it, but he was a pretty good hand and felt comfortable doing what he was doing. Riding sidesaddle and riding backwards in the saddle were only a few of his antics.

Our crew during the 2008 season was pretty good. They all got along well and there was a lot of practical joking going on among them. I had to caution them a time or two about this so as it wouldn't overflow and possibly endanger our customers.

TR Loren Schmidt

The crew that year consisted of Megan, Mandy, Shennon, Travis, Jason, Kevin, Josie, and me.

One day, Cuddles came in rider-less. There was a rush among the hands to catch and bridle their horses and ride out to see what happened, or to even possibly rescue Travis.

Jason was having a hard time getting on his horse. Megan and Mandy had caught up Cuddles, and Shennon had already got her horse and was headed up the trail when Travis appeared, leading his ride in on foot. Jason still hadn't got on his horse.

Jason was a big guy, and was pretty green when he first showed up. He was big enough that he had a problem getting on his horse. I had to give him a few lessons on how to get on a horse, and even then he still had some problems coordinating his movements.

As I was watching him trying to get on his horse to rescue Travis, I had the thought, "He might never get it right." Then I noticed that his stirrups seemed to be extremely short. His stirrups were way too short! Shennon had shortened his stirrups by about five holes! Jason would never get on with the stirrups that short.

Then Travis came walking in, leading the ride on foot with Shennon horseback, right behind him.

When the excitement died down, Travis explained that Cuddles hadn't bucked him off. He had got off to pick up a camera or something and hadn't kept a hold of Cuddles. The horse then simply decided to come home!

Aromas

I hired Fernando one spring to do our cooking, not only at the house, but also to do our breakfast and steak-fry rides. He was a good cook, and I never could figure out how he could tell medium rare from well done just by touching the steak. I didn't ask questions. I let him do the cooking, that wasn't my job. I just enjoyed the results of his labors.

Fernando was a good cook, not only on the cookouts, but at the house. However, he did tend to be a little forgetful. For the cookouts I would generally send him to the cookout grounds in the truck with the groceries before I sent the guests out. Then, for the steak-fry rides, the last ride of the day, I would unsaddle horses, feed, and then ride my horse to the cookout grounds to get my supper. This arrangement worked out pretty good, the hands liked it, and most of the evening chores were done when the steak ride was over.

My truck broke down, nothing real serious, but up here in Grand County, Colorado, if parts are needed for truck repairs, it generally requires an overnight stay for the truck while the parts are shipped up from Denver. Such was the case with my truck. This wasn't too serious, although we did have a cookout that night.

I could handle the situation. I'd let Fernando use my town car to do the cooking chores. It might be tough to get all the groceries and cooking utensils in the car, but even if Fernando had to make two trips, he could handle it. I'd got this car just to use as a town car—to get groceries, get the mail, and do other errands. And it was better on gas than the truck.

We got Fernando headed out on the cookout, and it was a success. We got the guests loaded on their horses and returned to the stables, leaving Fernando to clean up. It wasn't a tough job, just gather up the garbage in plastic sacks and put them in the dumpster at the stables.

I was in the barn, helping unsaddle horses when Fernando returned. I assumed Fernando got all the chores done and we headed home.

I got the truck out of the shop the next day, and work proceeded as normal. For some reason or another, I didn't use the car for a few days, but when I did, I noticed a strange odor. In fact, the car stunk!

I couldn't figure it out. I rolled all the windows down, didn't use the heater or air conditioning, but it didn't help. The car continued to stink and it got worse every day! I even bought some air fresheners and that didn't do anything. I looked under the car, thinking maybe I had hit a rabbit or something and it was lodged on the frame of the vehicle raising a stink. I couldn't find anything and the rotten smell was getting stronger and worse every day.

I got a flat tire going to work one day, and I actually felt some relief to get out of the stinking car even if I had to change a tire. When I opened the trunk, I found the cause of the smell. Fernando had forgotten to take the trash from the cookout out of the trunk! All that trash had been sitting there, cooking in the afternoon heat, day after day, raising a grand stink!

It didn't take me long to change the tire, get to the stables, and put the garbage in the dumpster. After that, it was almost a pleasure to drive to work!

Turn-About's Fair Play

My son Ben rides a few saddle broncs. He got interested in bronc riding while he was helping me at my rental horse stable in Granby, Colorado. He got interested in rodeo while guiding tourist rides at the stable and watching his older brother, Will, ride bulls at the local rodeos in Granby and Fraser.

Ben was interested enough that he got into the high school rodeo and got on the rodeo team. He's a pretty fair bronc rider and actually won the Colorado State High School Rodeo Saddle Bronc Championship in 1994.

My granddaughter, Jade, was eight years old in 2009. Ben was still riding saddle broncs and really liked the Rooftop Rodeo in Estes Park, Colorado. Jade and her mother had moved from Ohio to Loveland, Colorado, the previous winter and seeing as Jade had never seen a rodeo before, I thought I would take her to her first rodeo to watch her uncle ride. Besides that, I always enjoyed watching my kids ride.

I met Jade and her mom in the stands, then went behind the chutes to look for Ben. He had a good way to drive and because he had been late last year at this rodeo, he'd had his bronc turned out. He was notorious for "photo finishes"—showing up just in time to saddle his horse and ride.

On this particular night, Ben made one of his "photo finishes," much to the consternation of his old man. I was behind the chutes, trying to help him and trying to stay out of the way. I guess as these kids get older, they don't need much help from the old man anymore.

Ben got on his horse, called for the gate, and his rodeo was on! His horse came out fairly strong, but seemed to weaken, and Ben fell off!

I was all set to start bragging to Jade what a good bronc rider her uncle was, almost as good as her grandpa used to be, and Ben fell off! It kinda took the wind out of my sails.

Ben came back to the chutes with a big grin on his face.

"What happened?" I asked.

"I fell off a horse that didn't even buck," answered Ben, still grinning.

I almost replied, "You fell off a horse that even I could have rode!" But I kept my mouth shut. I'd put myself in that trap before.

We decided to leave the rodeo early. Ben had to go to Laramie to make another rodeo the next day and I had to work, but Jade talked me into letting her ride the mechanical bull. I was surprised she wanted to, but secretly proud she wanted to.

She did all right riding the mechanical bull, and was all set to come to Moraine Park to ride some broncs herself. Of course, we don't have any broncs at the stable, but she was ready. She promised that the following Sunday she'd bring her mom out and go for a ride.

On Sunday, Jade and her mom showed up, ready to go riding. I picked a horse for her, Ol' Sarge, a good, gentle horse that would carry anybody.

R. LOREN SCHMIDT

We started out and when we had got about a quarter of a mile from the barn, Jade asked, "Where are we going today, grandpa?"

"Well darlin'," I replied, "I really hate to tell you this, but ever since we started out, we've been headed back! An' we got two hours to do it in!"

It took her a minute to get it, but she just grinned and kept on riding. It was an uneventful ride, other than my teasing Jade fairly regularly, and there was plenty of that for two hours.

When we got back to the stables, I congratulated Jade on what a good bull rider she was and how she could probably do it again.

I picked her up and gave her a hug, then told her, "Next time you see your Uncle Ben, you tell him that you went for a horseback ride with your grandpa for two hours, but Ben couldn't stay on his horse for eight seconds!"

Language Barrier

Doing sleigh rides for the tourists in the winter can be pretty cold, but I always liked the money it provided. Sometimes it meant the difference between going hungry and sitting down to a good hot meal at night. And I always felt sorry for the horses coming in late at night with the steam just rolling off them. But, Mother Nature had provided for them better than me.

One night, we had a sleigh ride with a group of young adults from Japan. None of these folks spoke English, but they did have an interpreter with them. I gave them their instructions, like staying on the sleigh and not throwing things at the horses and the like, pausing after each item so the interpreter could pass on the instructions.

We started out, but I felt something was wrong! On most sleigh rides there's a lot of noise, people singing songs, telling jokes, asking questions about the horses and the like, but on this ride there wasn't a sound. Quite often, the guests would ask if they could sing, and my standard answer was, "Sure. But you need to sing the horse's favorite song."

"What's that," they would reply, "Jingle Bells?"

"No," I would answer, generally thinking it wouldn't bother me if I never heard "Jingle Bells" again. "The horses favorite song is a little known number titled, 'She Was Only a Stableman's Daughter, But All the Horsemen Knew Her.'"

This was an old joke, but it always brought a laugh. One group, a family reunion, returned the following year with words to the seemingly unknown song. I wish I had written those lyrics down; they were really funny, but not quite appropriate for all groups.

But this group had me concerned. They hadn't uttered a word, and I was wondering if they were having a good time or not. In an effort to assess the situation, I asked the interpreter, "Are these folks havin' a good time?"

"Yes," he replied, after looking the folks over. He seemed to think everything was okay.

"Do you think if I told a little joke an' you interpreted it, these folks might have a little better time?" I asked. "Perhaps," he replied.

So, I told a joke. I don't remember which one, but it was a pretty fair joke. And I was real careful to pause frequently so the interpretation could be done correctly and still not ruin the punch line. When I got to the end of the joke and the interpreter had finished, I was greeted with howls of laughter and even some applause.

I felt pretty good. This group was loosening up some and it is important to have fun on a sleigh ride. I was even starting to have fun.

"I'll tell another one if you'll interpret," I told the interpreter.

He said he would, and I started telling another joke, a better one than the last one, I thought. I was again careful to pause for the interpreter and all went well. I got to the punch line, expecting to hear howls of laughter and some more applause, but I didn't hear a sound. I was shocked!

"How come," I asked, "I heard a lot of laughter after I told the first joke, then I tell a second joke, even funnier, and I don't hear anything?"

The interpreter replied, "I told them to laugh after the first one!"

I could almost hear the horses laugh as I decided to cease trying to entertain this group.

The Right Horse for the Right Rider

Rocket was half Appaloosa, half draft horse. He was fairly large, but not really big. His markings weren't Appaloosa and not really typical of any of the draft horse breeds, just kind of a nondescript roan horse. In a herd of horses, a feller wouldn't pick him out as a good prospect for a saddle horse.

But Rocket was worth his weight in gold. He could be used as a kid's horse—he was plumb gentle—and he'd just follow along in line and never cause a problem. Plus he was stout enough to carry some pretty big people.

We had a large woman come to the stable with her family to go riding. The whole family was large and I had some misgivings about whether or not we could get them all mounted on safe, reliable horses. The woman was the real problem. She was about as wide as she was tall. Although she wasn't all that tall, she was plenty wide. I thought she probably exceeded our weight limit.

As I assigned horses, the short, obese woman was foremost in my mind. What horse could I put her on? I'd used most of my big horses for other members of the family, and my concern for a horse for the big woman was growing.

R. LOREN SCHMIDT

Not only did I need a big horse for the woman, I needed one with a saddle that had a big seat and stirrups that would shorten up enough to accommodate the big woman with the short legs.

Rocket! The horse popped into my mind like a bolt of lightning. The perfect horse! My concern became the saddle. Would the stirrups shorten up enough?

As I led the lady up to Rocket, I explained that this horse would be perfect for her, if I could get the stirrups short enough.

"He certainly looks big," the woman said. "Can I pet him?"

"Ask him," I said.

I started helping the rest of the crew put the riders on their horses, saving the large, but not tall, woman for last. We put her son, also a big person, on Snowflake, a Percheron draft horse. Snowflake was large enough to carry the woman, but was so wide, the woman's legs would have stuck straight out like she was riding a three-foot-wide ironing board. She wouldn't have been able to use her feet for balance at all if she had been riding Snowflake.

"Do you want me to be nice to you?" I asked her as I readied myself to get her on her horse.

"Oh yes!" was the reply. I imagine Rocket looked pretty big to her, as short as she was, although Rocket wasn't that big. "I don't think I can get on by myself."

I shortened the stirrups as much as I could and hoped they would be short enough.

"Then step over behind that mounting block an' stay on the grass behind it." I don't tell people to get on the block until I have the horse in place. If the person is standing on the mounting block when the horse is led to the block, the person looks larger to the horse, and I might never get the horse in position. I always think the horse might see how big the person really is and decide not to carry that particular person. Those dude horses get pretty wise pretty quick.

I got Rocket into position and told the lady to get on. I was really glad I'd shortened the stirrups before the lady got on—with all that weight in the saddle, I'd never have gotten the stirrups pulled down far enough.

Everybody was mounted, and after some brief instructions on how to handle a horse, we started out. Dave, the boss, had selected me to lead the ride, and he put the obese woman right behind me, with her son on Snowflake right behind her. I figured Dave thought their might be some problems with this woman, so he put her up behind me hoping I could prevent any misfortune. I keep a pretty close eye on the dudes when I'm on a ride.

I kept a pretty close watch on the woman and the other riders. The woman's son, on Snowflake, was rocking back and forth, from side to side, every time the horse put his foot down. I had to holler at him a time or two, and tell him to just sit on the horse. If he got to rocking back and forth, he might just rock himself off the horse.

I didn't have to worry much about the woman—every time Rocket put a foot down, she just settled into the saddle a little further. After a two-hour ride, I figured we'd have to get a crowbar and a backhoe just to get her out of the saddle!

The ride was uneventful, although I was almost hoarse from telling her son to sit straight. I had a kink in my neck from looking back, trying to keep him straight in the saddle. I certainly didn't want him to fall, but if he did, I wanted to see it!

All ended well, and Rocket, because he did such a good job, got the day off the next day. He carried a lot of weight and did it real well. But I had to work.

The Cook

Jeannie came to us in the spring of 2005. She really wanted to be a wrangler, but she was more suited to the cooking job and we already had plenty of wranglers. So she started cooking. She did get a chance to ride, generally taking out the eight o'clock or the 10:30 ride.

The meals went pretty good, meat and taters mostly, but a guy could get by on it. I sure wasn't doing any complaining, the cooking was a lot better than what I could do. After she'd been here a while, and gotten comfortable with the budget she had to work with, she started to experiment a little. We had a little more variety.

Everyone was getting used to a little variety and looking forward to mealtimes. The most common question asked was, "What's for supper?"

"I don't know," was Jeannie's reply.

One night, after a particularly hard day, Jeannie had fixed the regular meat and taters supper. It was kinda quiet at the supper table that night. Jeannie had fixed the taters with the skins on them and they were sorta mashed and sorta not mashed.

"Its kinda flat, isn't it?" Jeannie was concerned about the reaction to her supper.

"What's flat?"

Everyone looked at Jeannie, not wanting to say something inappropriate.

"Supper," replied Jeannie. "It's just really flat."

"No it isn't, Jeannie," I said. "You can see the lumps in the taters!"

My comment brought a pretty good laugh and every time Jeannie fixed the taters in that way, Dave, the manager, would say, "We've got lumpy potatoes again!"

Jeannie would always try to please. She asked everyone what their favorite supper was, and what their least favorite meal was. When she asked me, I told her, "I am good with meat an' taters anytime. Most of us old cowboys ain't too hard to please, an' don't take to change too well. As far as my least favorite, spaghetti don't set good with me." Jeannie was kind enough to fix spaghetti on my day off, when I'd generally eat in town.

One day, Jeannie fixed a homemade, made from scratch, cake. She made a big deal of it, and it did look good there in the middle of the supper table. Everybody was sorely disappointed when she cut it and the dough just oozed out on the platter. It hadn't cooked clear through! She wouldn't let anyone have any, as she had used fresh eggs to make the cake dough. I did manage to scrape a finger across the top and get some icing before she tossed it into the garbage.

The next night, Jeannie had another cake on the table. Before I sat down to eat, I noticed a fly buzzing menacingly around the table, so I got a fly swatter down off the wall just to be prepared.

"What are you doing?" Dave was curious.

"There's a fly close to the table," replied Jeannie.

"I figured I'd get him," I said.

"You don't have to worry," said Dave. "If he lands in the cake he'll probably drown!"

Jeannie had a particularly tough time cooking at high altitude. She knew I was really fond of banana cream pie, but she never could get it quite right. She couldn't get the banana cream to set up. Every time she fixed it, the banana cream just came running out.

The last time she fixed it, she brought it out with the comment, "If this didn't turn out, it's the last time I'm fixing it for you, Stu!"

"What is it?"

"Your favorite, banana cream pie."

"Do we need spoons or a straw to eat it? The last time we had it, it slouched right down the front of my shirt! It even soaked through!" I was beginning to have fun with Jeannie's banana cream.

"Better take a spoon, Stu," said Dave. "Take a fork, too! You can slow it down with the fork while you bail it out with the spoon!"

Spices also gave Jeannie some problems. She fixed something one day, I forget exactly what it was, but it sure was hot.

"Does this seem a little hot to you, Stu?"

"What did you put in this, Jeannie?" Dave asked, as beads of sweat were starting to emerge on his bald head.

"It does seem a little warm," I replied as Dave wiped the sweat off his head. "I ain't sweatin' yet, but my eyes are startin' to water!"

Jeannie also had some problems with her horses. One little black and white paint filly she was riding gave her a real tough time leaving the stable. No one else had a problem getting the horse to leave, but Jeannie had a lot of difficulty. It seemed like she didn't want to get tough and discipline the horse, she liked her too much.

The horse also tried to buck some with her, but I never saw it. In fact, the horse had gotten so fat from just standing around, I very seriously doubted if the little mare could buck at all.

I suggested to Dave that we let her use one of the good old rental horses, like Penny, rather than having her ride the younger horses that still needed some education.

Dave's reply was simple, "That filly is part of Jeannie's education."

"That filly might be part of Jeannie's education," I thought, "but I'll bet that horse can't teach her how to make banana cream pie not runny!"

Memory Loss

I was visiting with some of our guests while watching our wranglers picking out horses for their ride. I always enjoyed talking with our customers and I could keep an eye on the help and make sure they had the right kind of horses. It's really important to put the big people on the big horses, the kids on the kid's horses, and to make sure we didn't over-mount somebody.

The help was new, and it's real important to make sure the same horse doesn't repeatedly go out. The horses need a rest and a chance to get some feed and water in-between rides. Sometimes I'd have to holler precise instructions to the help as I visited with the folks. Precise instructions like, "No. That's a bay. Graham's is buckskin! He's got 638 branded on his hip." Or, "Don't tie Colby! He's a pullback!" Or, "Don't catch Scar. That's my horse. I'll get him later!" I had to be patient and give the new help a chance to learn the horses.

Sometimes a customer would comment, "Do you know everyone of these horses' names?"

"Yep," I would reply.

"Isn't it hard to learn all their names? How many horses are out there?"

"Nope," I would answer. "How many friends do you have? Do you know all their names? There are about ninety horses."

As they pondered my answer, I would think, "Yes, it's necessary to know all their names, but it's more important to know their personalities."

"I suppose it takes a lot of experience to do this job." An elderly gentleman made the comment.

"Yep," I replied. But I thought to myself, "Sometimes I wonder how much it takes to work here!"

"You certainly look like a real cowboy," continued the gentleman.

I didn't take that as a compliment. After saddling sixty or seventy horses in the morning and feeding them, it was hard to look like a prosperous businessman.

"Yep," I replied. "But that's a rather inglorious end to a feller whose parents had high aspirations of their son becoming the President or at least an important Senator."

"I suppose you've probably forgot more about these horses than these kids will ever know," answered the gentleman.

This comment was obviously a reference to my advanced age, but I passed over an excellent opportunity to expound on my horse knowledge at the expense of my relatively inexperienced hired help. I certainly didn't want to downgrade the help in front of the customers.

"There's not a day goes by that I don't fail to learn something new about these horses," I replied. "But at my age, I don't know if I knew it before an' had forgotten it, or if it really is new!"

The old man grinned and shook his head in quiet agreement. "I know the feeling," he answered.

Questions

I'm always kinda amused and sometimes amazed at the questions that are asked by the dudes, that is, the tourists. Sometimes, I like to get the jump on them.

For example, when a family comes up to the office to inquire about horseback rides, I like to change the standard greeting from, "Hello, can I help you folks?" to "Are you the people they sent to clean the corrals?"

This generally gets a good laugh, but invariably the parents volunteer the kids to do the job. Many parents reply, "I've done plenty of that in the past!"

My response is simple. "That's good! Having some prior experience is desirable. You can do the job better an' quicker!"

Still, the parents volunteer their children. Many times I've had to grab a kid to keep him from walking into the corral. They are willing, but they don't have any tools, such as a shovel or wheelbarrow. But it does make for some fun.

Sometimes they will ask, "What does the job pay?"

"It don't pay much," I reply. "But you can have all the horse manure you want!"

The thought of driving home with a trunk full of horse manure on a hot day is not really appealing to most folks, so we are stuck with cleaning the corrals ourselves.

Another question I've always enjoyed is, "Have you lived here all your life?"

"Not yet!" My reply is simple, yet it seems to create an awkward moment for the dudes until they realize their question is somewhat awkward. When they finally realize I'm answering their question honestly and not giving them a smart-aleck answer, they generally have a good laugh.

I used to give the same "not yet" answer to the question, "Have you been a cowboy all your life?" However, I had a lot of different people asking me the same two questions and I didn't want to repeat myself, so I started to change the answer.

When asked, "Have you been a cowboy all your life?" I would answer, "If the truth were known, no. I'm actually a former Enron executive up here hidin' out from the government. Pretty good disguise, ain't it?" Most folks can see that I'm just fooling with them and have a good laugh.

The dudes aren't the only ones that can ask questions. *I've* had a lot of fun asking the questions. When we have a group of people out by the rail, I'm asking the folks the questions, trying to match up the rider with the right horse. Before we even start I will pick out some of the ladies and ask, "Will you hold my hand for a good horse?"

I am surprised when the ladies reply, without any hesitation, "Yes!" Some of the gals just step up and grab my hand, some quite emphatically.

"Will you give me a hug for a better horse?" This second question generally brings a more enthusiastic reply.

"Certainly!" The reply is generally most affirmative. Some of the gals don't verbally respond, they step right up and give me a hug, sometimes with a little too much enthusiasm! But it does make for a good time.

Kids are sometimes a problem. Most kids want to pick the horse they want to ride and they pick the horse on color more than anything else. I prefer to pick the horse based on the disposition and dependability of the horse for all riders.

So when the question, "Do we get to pick our own horse?" arises, my standard reply is, "It's our policy to let you pick the horse you want to ride, an' we will let you ride the horse you pick, as long as it's the same horse we pick for you to ride."

The kids are generally pleased with this answer even though it's a nice way to say "No." Parents are generally amused by it also.

All in all, we can have a lot of fun with the dudes. And a smile or a laugh can do a lot to ease the individuals that are a little nervous or apprehensive about riding a horse.

I like to assign the youngsters their horses first, just to make sure there are enough good, dependable horses for the kids.

Often, I'll take a little girl and say, "Here, Darlin', hold my hand. We'll go get a good horse for you."

Usually, even the most timid, shy, bashful little girl will take my hand as we go to get her a horse.

As we walk off, hand in hand, I'll turn back to the parents and say, "This is the only way I can get the girls to hold on to me!"

This is always good for a laugh. Unfortunately, it's true.

Trying to Help?

Sometimes it can be difficult to get someone on a horse. Most of the time it can be done fairly easily, but every now and then a feller just wants to be helpful even if the person doesn't need help.

Such was the case with a newlywed couple that came to our stable for a horseback ride one day. When I found out they had only been married a couple of days, I had a lot of fun with them. They had a good sense of humor and I really enjoyed joking with them.

Of course I had to ask the new husband, "Have you been married long enough to know about the three rings of marriage?"

"Three rings of marriage—what's that?"

"Well," I said, "there's the engagement ring."

The new bride proudly held out her left hand and pointed to a big, shiny diamond.

"I can see you're already familiar with the first ring. The second ring is the wedding ring."

The new bride still had her hand out and proudly pointed to the gold band next to the diamond.

"What's the third one?" The new husband was anxious to fill his role as a husband.

"The third one is the suffer-ring!"

The new husband let out a hearty laugh, but I thought the new bride was going to brain me, but I did see a frown work itself into a smile as I took them out to their horses. They were a good couple.

"Here, young man," I said. "You ride this horse we call Widowmaker!" We didn't really call the horse Widowmaker, his real name was Grant. I heard the new bride laugh when I told her husband the fake name.

"And you, young lady, you ride this horse we call Sudden Death!"

The new husband was still laughing as I told the new bride that the real name of the horse was Solo.

One of my hired hands moved in to help the young lady get on her horse.

"Help the young man," I said as I tightened the cinch. "I'll help this young lady.

"Are you ready?"

The gal nodded her head.

"Then step right over here."

The new bride stepped into place and started to put her foot into the stirrup.

"Hold on now," I said.

The gal stopped.

"I'll help you get on, if you do everything exactly the way I tell you to do it. Can you do that?"

"Okay," she replied.

"Then put your left arm around my shoulder."

Obediently, she put her left arm around my shoulder.

"Now," I said, "the idea is to get you on this horse without fallin', right?"

She nodded her head, somewhat apprehensively.

"Okay, now put your right arm around my other shoulder."

She put her right arm around my other shoulder. Her new husband was already on his horse and he had an amused look on his face as he watched the proceedings.

The gal had both her arms around me, so I told her, "Now hold on tight. We don't want to drop you!"

The new bride is really giving me a good hug.

"Now wait a minute here, young lady," I said. "Quit huggin' me an' get on your horse!"

Starting to blush a little, the new bride let go and got on her horse.

I turned to her husband and asked, "What do you think of your new bride huggin' an ugly old cowboy like me?"

"That's all right, she's going home with me!" He had a big grin on his face.

Everybody had a good laugh, but I do think the new bride tried to kick me as I adjusted her stirrups.

Work Ethics

Finding good hired help is always a big task. There are always plenty of people looking for work, but trying to pick those individuals that can and will do the work at the standard we expect is a tough chore. I really don't think the work is that hard, although the days can be long. I've always had a hard time reconciling long days or long hours in my own mind. Each day is twenty-four hours long and each hour consists of sixty minutes. No one day or hour is any longer than any other. The difference amounts to what we can accomplish during any given day or hour.

At the Moraine Park Stables, outside Estes Park, Colorado, the work day routine is pretty simple. Barn call is around six o'clock in the morning. The crew will halter all the horses in the night corral. The horses will be let into a holding pen that leads into the barn. We have a saddling chute where the horses will enter the barn. Then they are brushed, a nose bag with grain will be put on them, and saddle blankets and pads are put on. Then they are saddled and the cinches are pulled just tight enough to hold the saddle in place. If a saddle is missing a raincoat, it's tied on.

The horses are then let out into a holding pen where they finish their grain. As they are let into the day pen, the nose bags are taken off. We generally have somewhere between eighty or ninety horses and we'll usually saddle sixty or seventy head. Some horses are given a day off because they might have a saddle sore or a cinch sore, or they might show signs of illness—maybe they're breathing a little irregular, or they're nose might be running. If they're not up to par, they're not used. Some horses, particularly the older ones, might get a day off simply because they worked the day before.

We can saddle the horses we need every day in about an hour. After saddling, the barn is cleaned, nose bags are filled for the evening, and we start getting horses out on the rail for the first ride of the day.

The rides are staggered throughout the day. The two-hour rides leave at eight, ten-thirty, one-thirty, and four o'clock. Longer rides leave at eight and one o'clock. Occasionally, we can send out rides at times other than our established ride times during the afternoon, as long as we have enough help to cover our reservations later in the day. When the first ride has left, the horses that were on the rail and not used are turned loose, the morning hay is put out, and any chores that were not completed are done.

There's not much to do between rides except to clean the rail area, mend equipment, just in general what I call "rat-killing."

I don't think the work is all that hard. It is a little stressful out on the ride, trying to keep it safe and not letting any of the dudes fall off. It's been my experience that when someone falls off, it's their own fault. They're not following instructions.

The last ride of the day leaves at four, consequently it's back to the barn at six. The evening feeding has been done, and when the four o'clock ride returns, the horses are unsaddled, grained, and turned into the night pen. The barn is cleaned, and our day is done. To me, it's a pretty simple day.

But, finding help to do this is a really tough part of the management job. Today people just want to get a paycheck and not do much to earn it.

I'm always leery of prospective employees who, after hearing a brief job description, ask, "When is payday?" I always thought people of this ilk were just interested in the money and not in how well they could do the job. Payday will always come even though some of the employees aren't worth their pay.

If a person doesn't know much about horses but shows an inclination to learn, we can generally hire that individual and teach him or her.

Such was the case with Megan and Mandy. These two girls came together from Iowa where they were college students. They came in pretty green, not having much horse experience. However, we do have some training sessions and these girls listened and paid attention and learned. As a result, they turned out to be real good help and I came to depend a great deal on them.

This was not the case with all individuals. Dave, our stable manager, hired a guy from Arizona who had very limited experience. He had worked for two or three weeks at the stable in Phoenix and had just buffaloed his way through his time there. But he didn't know much and he didn't show much inclination to learn more.

During one training session, he kept interrupting, trying to be helpful I think, with comments like, "Down in Arizona, we do it this way."

It was becoming very difficult to continue the training session with the constant interruption. Finally, becoming very frustrated, I said, "Whose doin' this trainin'? If you want to do things the way they do it in Arizona, you can go to Arizona an' do it down there! I'm showin' everyone how to do it here!"

I've worked at the same stable he worked at in Arizona and their system works well for them, but our facility is different and our system works well at our location.

I lost my temper with this guy and felt kinda bad about it, so I got him alone and tried to explain how and why our system works. I finished by saying, "The mark of a good hand is to be able to go to other outfits an' adapt to their way of doin' things. The means may be different, but the result is the same."

I thought I had the situation well in hand, and there was some improvement in his attitude. But he was still trying to teach without having the proper knowledge or experience.

It wasn't too many days later when we were discussing things that he made the statement, "You know, my ol' Gran-pappy used to say, 'The mark of a good hand is to be able to go to other outfits an' adapt to their way of doin' things.'"

"I wonder where I've heard that before," I said.

"Did you know my ol' Gran-pappy?" he asked.

He was still trying to buffalo his way through. And it is his nature to try to convince everyone he knows it all regardless of how much he actually does know.

I know I had to correct him one morning while we were saddling. He didn't want to take my corrections and started to argue with me. I got a little peeved and hollered at him to "just do things my way and shut up!" After some muttering, he did just that.

Dave came around the corner and made the comment, "Thirty years worth of experience isn't worth much these days."

All I could do was grin.

This particular individual, for all that he did or didn't know, had a hard time tightening cinches just tight enough to hold the saddle in place. One morning we looked out in the day corral and there were four or five horses with saddles rolled under their bellies. I had tried to show this feller just how tight to pull the cinches, but he either just didn't get it or he wasn't paying attention.

This was Travis' second year working for us and he went out and re-saddled those horses whose saddles had rolled. I could see he was upset, but didn't have a chance to talk to him, and he just gathered up his stuff and quit. Our know-it-all hand not only didn't know it all and caused us more work, but he had succeeded in running off a pretty good hand that didn't need constant supervision.

Then, to make matters worse, along about the middle of July, when he was starting to make a fair hand, he gave us a week's notice and left. This left us short-handed the rest of the summer and we actually would have been better off if he had never been hired!

Dave made the comment that he had never had much luck with people he had hired from Arizona and he might not hire any more from Arizona.

We had another gal that summer that was a real piece of work. She was heavy and more interested in throwing knives and tomahawks than working with horses. She would have been more at home at a mountain man convention than a rental horse stable. She was also quite argumentative. After some heated arguments with Dave about the horse she should ride and the rides she should take, she was transferred to another stable. I was glad to see her go.

Before she was transferred, she would bring her friends up on her day off and take them into the corral to show off her guide horse. I was raised with the idea that a person never stepped into another man's corral unless he was invited.

I set her down one day and explained to her that it was a matter of common courtesy to let the barn boss know what she and her friends were doing in the corral on her day off.

"But I work here."

Her reply didn't hold much water. On her day off, she wasn't working here.

I also told her that only employees were allowed in the corral.

"But they're with me."

"It doesn't make any difference," I replied. "We need to maintain some control here or we could get someone hurt. It's also a matter of common courtesy."

Common courtesy is an aspect of today's young people that seems to be missing. The young lady's behavior didn't change. Yes, I was glad to see her go.

That same year we had one feller that was very slow. No matter what I said or did, I couldn't get him to hurry up. Saddling in the morning, I could saddle two horses to his one. I made the comment to someone that he was real slow.

"No. He's just deliberate," was the reply.

"You're right," I said, "deliberately slow!"

This slowness was evident in everything he did, but he could ride, so he was kept on.

We had one girl that made me think of an old yeller horse that Emory Smith had over in Utah. This horse was an old pensioner that Emory was just letting retire. He kept the horse in a small pasture in front of the ranch house.

The horse would lie down, and then start to graze. When he got all he wanted in one spot, he'd get up, move to another spot, lie down, and start to graze again.

Emory would see this and remark, "That's the height of laziness!"

I would see this gal and think of that old yeller horse. This gal's attitude was, "If I'm the last one out there, I won't have to do as much work."

I was told that she said exactly those same words early in the season. Her attitude all summer seemed to be just that. She was the last one to start any particular chore, except when the day was done and we started to the house to eat.

She also reminded me of a guy who was drafted into the army. He made sure he got twelve hours of sleep a day. I asked him why he slept so much.

"If I can sleep twelve hours a day, I only have to spend half my time in the army!"

Kind of humorous, but a really poor work ethic.

Is Right Wrong?

I did horse rides at The Big Corral by Vallecito Reservoir outside of Durango, Colorado, for a couple of summers. The trail was pretty simple—we went out, made a loop, and then came back on the same trail. The trail was about three miles long and we had to use about a mile of the same trail coming and going.

I used to tell the customers they got to see the country both ways, coming and going, to try and relieve the monotony. I didn't think the scenery was all that great, as the area had been hit by the Missionary Ridge Fire some years before and the area was covered by dead, blackened trees from that fire. It was interesting to see the new growth of the vegetation as Mother Nature restored herself. It was more readily apparent in the spring of the second year. The area was fast becoming an aspen jungle.

There was an Osprey nest at the top of a pine tree on the left side of the trail going out. The nest had been in use for years and the fire had mercifully spared the nest and tree. It was a big nest, probably four or five feet across.

Every now and then we could watch the adult birds bringing in a fish to feed their young. Later on in the summer, we could see the chicks' heads poking out above the nest. Later on, we got to watch the young birds taking their first tentative flights.

I thought the trail was sort of boring, so I would try to bring a little interest to the ride by pointing out various things. I was always careful to point out the Osprey nest.

"Look over there, on the left, at the top of that tree, there's a big Osprey nest!" I would holler this out real loud, so everyone on the ride would see it and remember it.

Farther up the trail, as we crossed over some little ridges, I would stop my horse, stand up in the saddle and try to appear as if I was seeing something ahead of me.

"Everybody, be quiet," I would say and try to whisper at the same time. "There's a big herd of them ahead of us. If you just keep your horses moving an' keep quiet, everybody will get to see them before they jump up an' run off!"

I was careful not to tell the folks what "them" was, and it was interesting to watch the dudes trying to stand up in the saddle, craning their necks to see what "them" was.

I would lead the ride around the ridge and stop again where everyone could see the opposite hillside.

"See them over there? They're still lying down, they haven't run off yet!"

The folks were straining, trying to see "them," and not knowing what "them" was—probably thinking that "them" was a herd of elk or something. All they could see was a hillside, covered with rocks and underbrush.

When everyone had a chance to look over the hillside and couldn't see what they were supposed to see, they would look to me, with a question on their faces, "Where are they?"

"See 'em?" I would say. "They're still there! They haven't spooked yet, they're still laying there!"

More questioning looks would come my way. Finally, when I would see some frustration directed my way, I would say, "They're

still there. See 'em? What, can't you see that herd of rocks lying on that hillside? They're still there, they haven't run off yet!"

The look of frustration on their faces quickly turned to a look of something else as they figured out that I had fooled them. I pulled this little stunt a lot and had a lot of fun doing it.

Probably the most fun I had was with Tommy. We had just hired Tommy, and it was my job to take him out with a ride and show him the trail. When I pulled this stunt, I could see Tommy standing in the saddle trying to see what "them" was, just like the dudes. He fell for this little ruse just like the dudes. I enjoyed that.

I took him on a ride later that afternoon, just to help watch the dudes. The trail was pretty simple, he should know it, but I had a big group.

I pulled this little stunt again, and I saw Tommy standing in the saddle again, trying to see what "them" was. Tommy had fallen for the stunt again! Twice in the same day! I really enjoyed that, but he never fell for it again!

Generally, the rides would be uneventful. When we merged into the trail to return to the stable, I would look to the right.

"Look," I would say. "There's another Osprey nest on the right!"

Invariably, the kids behind me would say, "That's the same one we saw earlier."

"No. Think about it. The first one we saw was on our left. This one's on our right, so it's another one. You guys have seen two Osprey nests today!"

"It's the same one!" Their reply would be quite adamant. "We're going a different direction!"

"No, no," I would reply. "We're still going forward, so it's a different nest!"

Regardless of how much the youngsters would argue, I would maintain that it was a different nest. Some of the youngsters would become quite frustrated at my seemingly lack of direction, but I would hold fast to my side of the argument. It was a lot of fun and I really don't know how many kids I actually convinced that they had seen two Osprey nests.

Sometimes right is wrong. Or, maybe right is left. I don't know.

A Journeyman

Our hired help at the Moraine Park Stables has a vast amount of varied experiences. Sometimes they don't have a lot of experience with horses, but if they are willing to learn and can apply themselves, we can generally teach them what they need to know to do the job we want them to do.

Such was the case with Kevin. He came to us the spring of the 2006 season. He had some experience with horses, but said he had a varied background. He did seem to be quite proud of the fact that he had done some carpentry work and stated that he was a "journeyman carpenter."

I took him at his word. When we had a door on the barn that was sticking, I assigned Kevin to the task.

"Do you think if we adjusted the rollers on the top of the door that it would roll along the rollers and be easier to latch?" I asked.

I thought that was the problem and Kevin seemed to agree. When he got a ladder and made the necessary adjustments, the door rolled easily and latched. My faith in Kevin's carpentry skills was justified. However, that was soon to be tested.

During the last part of May, before school lets out, it's a little slow business-wise. This is a good time to do some training and catch up with odd jobs. Quite often we do some painting on the buildings and corrals and get caught up with general maintenance.

Dave, our boss, had decided that we needed a new mounting block, as the one we had was starting to show its age. I kinda thought this might be along the lines of "busy work," but it probably needed to be done. This spring would be a good time to do it, as business was slow.

I thought Kevin would appreciate building a new mounting block. He could build it in the new barn where he would be out of the wind. It was still cold and the wind coming off the still snow-covered mountains made it even colder. I know I would have appreciated just getting in out of the wind, regardless of what I was doing, as long as it wasn't dishes in the kitchen.

I helped Kevin get what carpentry equipment we had. It wasn't much—a couple of saws, a hammer, some nails, and a tape measure. We don't have much use for finished carpenter's equipment.

"Kevin," I said, "what we need is a new mounting block. It needs to be a little bigger an' a little stronger than the old one."

Actually, it needed to be quite a bit bigger than the old one. I got a little nervous when I would see some of our larger riders balancing precariously on the old mounting block as we led their horses up to them. It was kinda humorous, but it was also an accident looking for a place to happen.

I helped Kevin get some plywood and some two-by-fours and two-by-sixes gathered up and into the barn.

"Yep," I thought, "this would be an excellent time to complete this little project. And to be in out of the wind where it was a little warmer would be a bonus."

I thought I could do the job in less than a day, but if it was still cold, I could stretch it into two days if I painted it. It would have to be painted. Two days out of that bitterly cold wind would be a bonus!

I made sure Kevin knew what we wanted, told him to do a good job and if we had any rides, we would come and get him. As I left, I partially closed the door, just to let in enough light so he could see what he was doing. I left him alone. I always think its best to leave someone alone when he's doing a job. I never like someone looking over my shoulder when I'm doing something, and besides, he was, by his own admission, a journeyman carpenter. He surely didn't need someone who didn't know what he was doing telling him what to do.

Kevin was on his own, and a couple of days later I asked him, "How's the mounting block coming? It should be done by now."

"It's coming," was his reply.

A couple of more days passed and I noticed he was spending a lot of his spare time visiting with the other hired help. We did use him when his turn came to take out some rides. That's when I looked in the barn and saw that there was a rough frame assembled, but it wasn't square. Quite a few days had passed since Kevin started this project, and by now it should have been done—painted and in use.

I told Kevin that this job had to be done by the next day and to get him going, I told him, "You're not goin' to take any rides until that mountin' block is done!"

Kevin figured himself to be a cowboy and it was kind of insulting to him that he wasn't going to ride until the mounting block was completed.

"What's takin' you so long on that mountin' block? I could have had it done last week!"

I saw a look on Kevin's face that seemed to say, "Then why don't you do it?"

"I don't have the right tools," replied Kevin.

"The right tools? What are the right tools? You have everything we have."

"I don't have a power saw or an air gun. And I really need those to do a good job." Kevin's answer seemed a little weak.

"My God! Noah didn't have an air gun or power saw when he built the ark! He just did it! You'll just have to do with what we have. We ain't goin' to get that fancy equipment just to do this simple little job. And it will have to be done by tomorrow!"

I was starting to get a little irritated. The only reason Kevin was doing this job was because he had led me to believe he was a journeyman carpenter and he was more qualified than anyone else to do it. He had been given—and had taken—more than enough time to do it.

The next day, right before noon, Kevin came to me and said, "I'm done."

"Well, let's go give it a test," I said.

Everyone who wasn't on a ride went to the barn to admire Kevin's new creation.

"Go ahead an' get on it," I said as we formed a semi circle around the new mounting block.

It wasn't done. Kevin had made some steps to get up on the platform, but he hadn't covered the sides with plywood. It was just a skeleton—and it wasn't square.

Kevin weighed about 180 pounds, maybe 190, maybe a little more. The mounting block made a creaking noise as Kevin stepped on the first step. As he stepped on the second step, the mounting block swayed a little and there was a louder creaking noise. Finally, he stepped onto the platform amidst the continued creaking and swaying.

I was becoming concerned. The mounting block would have to support a good deal more weight than Kevin. It would certainly have to be more solid. Some of our heavyweight riders exhibited some lack of balance when they got on our old mounting block.

"There," said Kevin. "Better than the old one!"

As he said that, he bounced up and down on the platform. Then it happened. He and the platform came crashing to the ground, much to the dismay and amusement of the spectators! Come to find out he had nailed the platform to the bottom of the frame!

Kevin was unhurt, but greatly embarrassed. We all had a good laugh at Kevin's expense.

The next day, while Kevin was out on a ride, Adam Brown and myself tore apart the mounting block and reassembled it. It was square, and braced properly. In the afternoon we painted it and put it in its place. It didn't make any noise—and still doesn't—when a person steps up on it.

Sometimes I'm amazed at what a couple of country boys can do, especially compared to what the so-called professionals can do. So much for journeymen!

Personality Conflicts

I've done a lot of hiring and firing in my tenure in the rental horse business. The hiring is done on a positive basis; I'm trying to hire people that can get along well with the general public and do the job expected of them. Firing people is generally done without much ceremony and as quickly as possible.

When hiring someone, I'm careful to stress to the prospective employee that there are only four things they need to do to keep management happy. Those four things are: First, take good care of our customers; second, take good care of our horses; third, take good care of our equipment, and fourth, get along with the rest of the hired help.

"If you can do these four things," I would tell the prospective employees, "you don't have to worry about keeping management happy. They will be happy as they can be."

Doing the fourth item, getting along with the hired help, proved to be the most difficult. Personality conflicts, particularly among the younger fellers always seemed to be present. Egos among young cowboys seem somewhat stronger than among other young people. The teenage cowboys, and even those in their early twenties, seem to have a "macho" or "John Wayne" image that they need to establish, maintain, and protect. Consequently, in protecting this "tough cowboy" image, a lot of young fellers got themselves into some pretty tricky situations, and a lot of them got bucked off their horses.

If I had my choice, I'd hire all girl crews. The gals are nicer to our customers, they treat our horses better, and they care for the equipment better. It doesn't bother them to sew up a hole in a nose bag in their spare time. Also, generally they're cleaner. They don't show up in the morning with a five-o'clock shadow.

I've been quite amused in the beginning of the season. The gals would show up in the morning with their hair done up proper and all their makeup in place. I noticed that it wasn't too many days later that a lot of the makeup disappeared and a cowboy hat ruled over fancy hair styles.

We had one feller, I'll call him Art, who had a good work ethic, but his personality was very abrasive. I never could figure out if he was actually trying to protect his cowboy image, if he was trying to hide the fact that he didn't know as much as he would have you believe he knew, if he was a little on the slow side, or if he was difficult to work with and he questioned almost every management decision that was made. Sometimes, he made the job harder. I worked with Art one summer and it was a relief when he left at the end of the season. I was actually looking foreword to the next season—I didn't think Art would be back, and the chances of getting someone with an abrasive personality like his were fairly slim.

We were short-handed the following spring and a few extra hands would be welcome.

"There'll be another hand showing up today," said Dave, the boss.

I tried to get some more information out of Dave, but he wouldn't say much, other than, "He's done some riding."

I was relieved to hear that. I was in charge of the training, and if this new hand had done some ranch work, I wouldn't have to do as much or as intensive a training session. It was starting to get busy and there wasn't much spare time for training.

We were having supper that night, when the door opened.

"Hello, Art!" Gabby voiced the greeting.

I had just started chewing a big piece of roast beef, and with it and my false teeth in my mouth, I almost choked!

"Art!' I didn't have to be told who the new hand was.

I looked at Dave sitting across the table. He was laughing heartily as he stood up to shake Art's hand. But his laugh was directed at me. And he was enjoying it.

Since Art had worked here before, he knew the routine. The next morning, after we saddled the horses and got the first ride on the trail, Dave called Art and me to the office. It was Dave's habit to bring in another person when he was about to discipline someone. This was for his and the company's protection. If there was some backlash later on, Dave would have a witness. As the barn boss, I was the witness.

"You and I have got crossways in the past, Art," Dave started. "I'm willing to overlook the past, but there are two things you have to watch in the future if you're going to work here. One is your nose; you have to keep your nose out of everyone else's business. The other one is your mouth; you have to keep your mouth shut!"

Art agreed to this, but because of his abrasive personality, I would have to remind him about once a week to mind his own business and to keep his mouth shut.

We got along pretty well that summer, better than the last season, but there was more trouble brewing.

We hired another hand, a feller that had also done some riding before. But this feller, I can't remember his name so I'll call him Joe, came with a reputation as a hard drinker.

We don't allow any alcohol or drugs on the place. Those items don't generally lend themselves to a good working environment.

With Joe's reputation having preceded him, Dave gave Joe and the rest of the crew a discussion about what was and was not acceptable at this stable.

Things went well for a few days, and then Joe went to town one night after work. I was told he was found on the pathway leading to the bunkhouse, passed out. He really wasn't in shape to guide any rides the next day, so he spent a lot of time cleaning the rail area and doing menial, rat-killing type jobs.

One night a few days later, Joe and Art had a very heated argument. Joe came up to me to voice his complaint about Art. I listened very quietly until Joe was done.

"I understand you were kinda drunk a few nights ago," I said.

"I drink," said Joe, "but it doesn't affect my work!"

I thought of Joe doing the rat-killing jobs the day before and how we couldn't use him to take out rides because he smelled of booze.

"Yes, it does," I thought.

Joe was continuing to rant on about Art. "He doesn't know what he's doing. He makes me nervous. I just can't work with him!"

I was already familiar with Art's faults, and Joe was listing them out, item by item, as if to justify his position. I just listened.

Joe continued, "He's just too tough to work with. He makes every job harder. I can't work with him! It's either him or me!"

This left me in a particularly tough spot. I didn't really care for either one of these guys. If I had had the help, I would have fired both of them. One had an abrasive personality and the other one was a drunk. But I was still short of help and really couldn't let either one of them go. And, I didn't want to be accused of running off the help when we were short handed.

When Joe said, "Its either him or me," I knew it would be Joe.

"Why don't you talk to Dave about this? He's the one that has the final say," I said.

I don't know if Joe went and talked to Dave or not. The next thing I knew was that Joe was walking down the road, his clothes in a plastic garbage bag.

Art stayed the rest of the season, even though I had to continually remind him to keep his mouth shut and his nose out of everyone else's business.

The following year, Dave told me that Art had called him.

"What for?" I was hoping Art wasn't looking for another job.

"He actually called to thank me for being so tough on him! He's got a job as a barn boss at another stable."

As time went on, I heard they had a lot of hired help problems at that other stable.

Sometimes the job ain't as hard as getting along with the hired help!

Hospitality

When I started my stable in Grand County, Colorado, I was approached by a realtor.

"How can I help you?" I had no idea how I could help him, other than selling him a guided trail ride, horseback. After all, that's what I was in business for.

He explained to me that he was Bill, with a time-share company, and wondered if I would be interested in attending a hospitality party that he put on every week for the tourists. He thought I could generate more business by showing up and letting his guests know what we did at the Broken Spur Stables.

I thought it might be a good idea and told him I would show up an' check it out.

"By the way," he added, "our activities people generally provide a door prize that we have a drawing for at the end of the meeting. You might want to give away an hour horseback ride."

"How about a two for the price of one horseback ride?" I didn't really want to give away anything as I was just getting started and money was kinda tight. Besides that, I always thought half of something was better than all of nothing.

He agreed to that and the next Sunday I went to my first hospitality party. I sorta felt out of place, dressed in my work clothes, big hat, and boots. I hadn't even cleaned off my boots—they were still covered in horse manure.

Sometimes, when trying to catch a particular horse, a feller has to move kinda fast and doesn't have a chance to watch where he's stepping.

I sat in the back of the room and watched the proceedings, feeling somewhat embarrassed. I listened as the other activities people got up and made their pitches. There were river rafting businesses, mountain biking businesses, all sorts of activities represented.

I noticed as the party dragged on that the number of guests began to dwindle. People were leaving! Being a new participant to this party, I knew my pitch was going to be last, if everyone hadn't left by the time they got to me. I decided I would just have some fun here and wouldn't give a dry, boring presentation.

Finally Bill said, "Now we'll have Stu come up and tell you about what he does."

"I ain't goin' to be up here long, 'cause I don't do nothin'. But I'm gettin' pretty good at it!"

This comment brought a good laugh that I hadn't really expected. I told a couple of jokes, then said, "Oh, by the way, we do one- and two-hour horseback rides for the tourists. We also offer a breakfast ride an' a steak ride, where we ride out for about an hour, get you off your horses an' feed you your meal. The cook is already there, got the fire goin' an' cooks your food the way you want it. Then we get you back on your horses, an' it's about a twenty minute ride back to the barn."

I went on and told them the prices and other pertinent information. I even went so far as to tell them that if they signed up at this party and paid me today, I'd give them a little discount. Then I asked for questions.

I was surprised at the number of questions there were regarding the steak ride. I answered questions about the menu: "Yes, it's USDA Choice beef top sirloin steak, cooked over an open fire the way you want it," I repeated the price again, the time it left, I answered every question.

"Any more questions? Then I guess I'm done."

A lady in the back raised her hand. "Tell us more about the steak ride," she asked.

I was at a loss as what to say. I thought I'd done everything necessary except eat their steak for them. So I started to ad-lib.

"This week, we'll have some of the best steak rides we've ever had simply because last week it was one of the best horses we ever had that died!"

That brought a good laugh and I went back to my chair. I was surprised at the number of people that came back and signed up for our rides. Even the lady that asked the last question signed her family up for a steak-fry ride.

These hospitality parties generated so much business that I had to make up a sheet with our departure times on it and be very careful taking reservations. I didn't want to over-book any of our ride times. We did have a customer-to-guide ratio that we had to maintain.

I was even more surprised when, on the evening of her ride, the lady walked up to me, plate in hand with a ten-ounce top sirloin steak on it, and asked, "Is this really horse meat?"

I almost choked on my own meal when she asked that! I thought I had made it clear it was USDA Choice top sirloin beef steak.

"No lady, it ain't really horsemeat," I said.

"Then what is it?"

"Actually, it's dead cow!"

She seemed satisfied.

The Naturalist

On a book-selling trip during the off-season in the fall of 2009, I stopped at a bookstore outside of Quartzite, Arizona. The place was operated by a nudist. All this guy wore was a thong, kinda like an old Bull Durham tobacco sack, over his private parts. The rest of him was butt naked. But, he did have a good tan.

The locals had gotten used to this individual and seemed to accept him and his ways. His fame as the "naked bookseller" had spread around the country, and people would travel for miles just to see him. He posed for quite a few photographs with the tourists—at no charge.

When I saw him, it brought to mind a feller we hired at the Moraine Park Stables a few years ago. This guy was a naturalist. He didn't walk around butt naked, but he did have a big interest in nature and the critters that inhabited the outdoors.

He wasn't too much of a horseman, but he could ride in a fairly acceptable fashion. His work was acceptable, but not all of it was done on a professional basis.

Quite often, when we sent him out as a leader on a two-hour ride, his rides would come back late. When we sent him out as a second guide on a larger ride, he and the people behind him, would come in late.

Whenever the rides came in late, I would become very concerned. I didn't know if someone had trouble with their horse, or if someone had fallen off. His rides arriving late caused me to have some very stressful moments.

"How come you're late? Did you have any problems? You're late by fifteen minutes! I've been very concerned."

"We saw a ..." Then he would rattle off the name of some bird or some other critter and describe it completely. I wasn't too interested in the birds, I was more concerned with the safety of our horseback riders and I was beginning to wonder if he was paying as much attention to our customers as he should have been.

This attitude flowed over into his other work. One morning when we were in the night pen haltering horses in preparation for saddling, I watched him observing some bird that had perched on a horse's rump.

He wasn't just watching the bird, he appeared to be studying the bird. And he studied the bird for a good ten minutes while I haltered four or five horses.

Knowing that the bird would fly off when I approached, I walked up and said, "Let's get these horses haltered. We've got plenty of time to watch the birds when our morning chores are done. I've haltered four or five horses in the time you've been watching that bird!"

He resumed haltering horses, but never did get as many haltered as the rest of the crew.

He left early that summer, before the end of the season. In his absence, the rides came in on time. The stress factor was greatly diminished on my part. He was seen along the trail occasionally, observing nature. At one point he was seen sun bathing on a rock. I never did hear if he had his clothes on or off.

Loren Schmidt

I was discussing this feller with the cook, Jeannie, one day after he left and Jeannie made the comment, "He certainly had a great interest in nature, didn't he? He really knew all the wildlife and all the plants. He was a real naturalist, wasn't he?"

"If he was such a naturalist," I said, "why didn't he ride in the nude?"

Jeannie blushed a little and left.

Hoolihan

The cold winds of approaching winter intermingled with a mixture of rain and snow does not make for a pleasant day. Such was the case a few years ago over by Craig, Colorado.

I was working for Sombrero Stables. I had been managing the horse rental stables in Grand Lake during the summer and now I was helping out in preparation for the fall elk and deer hunts.

Sombrero leases out a lot of horses for the hunting season. The hunters welcome the snow and colder weather, I don't. I don't like the cold. For some reason or other, it makes all the work a little harder. And there's a lot of work getting the horses ready for the hunters.

We had four or five horseshoers at Big Gulch, about twelve miles outside of Craig. They had plenty of work to do, pulling and resetting shoes on the rental horses.

Doug and I were given the job of keeping the horseshoers supplied with horses. This wasn't too tough—most of the horses we could just walk up to and catch. There were a few that were hard to catch and we'd have to corner them. It wasn't much fun trudging through the mud in the corrals leading a horse out.

If we could rope the horses, it would be easier. There wasn't so much walking.

"Why don't we just rope all of 'em? It sure would be a lot easier than walkin' through all this mud," I said.

"I guess we could do that," answered Doug.

"An' we could have a little fun. How's about we rope for a dollar a miss?"

"We could do that, but only up to ten bucks," replied Doug. Doug had a wife and a kid and really couldn't afford to run up a big gambling debt.

We went to our saddle horses and pulled down our lariat ropes. I was thinking, "It sure would be nice if we could tie our horses in the shed and keep 'em out of the rain an' snow." The snow was beginning to build up on our saddles, but the horse-shoers were in the shed and they were already crowded.

As we returned to the catch pen, we ran about thirty head of horses into the pen.

"Now we're goin' to hoolihan these horses, right?"

"Right," answered Doug. "But let's do it one at a time."

I had the strange feeling that maybe Doug didn't fully trust me. But that was all right. A feller needed a little room to throw the hoolihan.

The hoolihan is a real neat throw for catching horses. There's not a lot of swinging the lariat, which creates a whizzing sound that tends to get the horses running. The throw consists of one swing around the head, and then it's thrown, kinda like a baseball. It's quiet and real slick when it's done right.

Doug gave me the first throw and, surprisingly, I caught a horse. Then Doug took his turn and missed. His lariat rope landed in the mud. This wasn't good for Doug—his rope was lying in the mud and as the horses milled around, they were tromping his rope into the mud! The heavy wet clay soil stuck to his rope like bubble gum to the bottom of a boot.

As it turned out, nobody won any money that day. We both missed some throws, and after our ropes were thoroughly covered with mud, gave up on the idea of roping horses. It was harder to throw the heavy ropes than to walk out of the corral with a horse.

However … on that day I found out why I was such a lousy roper. No, it wasn't because the rope was too heavy. When I threw the hoolihan standing on the ground, I could get my body weight into the throw and send the loop out quite a way. I couldn't do that in the saddle.

Hats

Buying a new hat has always been a problem for me. I don't really care much for the Quarter Horse crown that is most popular these days. It seems like that particular style is all that's available in the western stores today.

I've been told that in the old days a feller could tell where someone was from by the kind of hat he wore. But that's not true today.

Some years ago, I decided to buy a new hat. Prices were quite a bit cheaper then. I found a western store that was having a sale on hats and thought I might save some money by getting one now. I had done quite a bit of shopping at this store and knew everyone that worked there.

I found a hat that fit and was admiring how well it fit in the mirrors.

A sales lady walked by and remarked, "You don't want to buy that hat, Stu!"

Puzzled, I asked, "Why? It fits."

"No, don't buy that hat!"

"How come? It fits," I said. "Besides that, it's on sale an' I got the twenty-five dollars it costs!"

"Well, it doesn't make sense."

"Doesn't make sense? We're not talkin' cents here, we're talking dollars! An' I got 'em."

"No," she said, "You don't want to buy the hat!"

"How come I don't want to buy the hat? I got the money, it fits, an' while I admit I don't do much for the hat, it does a lot for me!"

"No, you don't want to buy that hat! What's the sense in buying a twenty-five dollar hat and putting it on a two-bit head?"

I showed her—I bought the hat anyway.

I have three boys and when I had my horse rental stable in Grand County, Colorado, all three of the boys helped me out. They all wore black hats with the same brim and crown shape. The boys were all redheads and looked very much alike. I had a hard time telling them apart until they got up close. When they were leading rides in, I learned to tell them apart only by the horse each one was riding. That's a heck of a note with your own kids, but that's the way it was.

I got so tired of buying hats that everyone else was wearing that I decided to start having them custom made. The Quarter Horse crown was becoming boring to me, along with the black color. I'd quit buying black hats about twenty years ago. None of my kids had ever seen me wearing a black hat—I'd always wear a silver belly.

My oldest boy, Will, and I were discussing hats one day and Will made the comment, "You've never wore a black hat in your life!"

That night I pulled out an old photograph album and showed Will a picture of me in a black hat. I had owned one years ago when I was young and macho. But they're too hot and I'm not that macho anymore.

A good friend of mine in Wyoming was ordering his hats from a company that only made custom hats. I got a copy of their catalog and an order blank and made my hat specifications the way I wanted it. I picked out the crown size and shape, brim size and shape, and the color.

I made out a check and sent in my order, then anxiously awaited the arrival of my new hat. I kinda felt like a kid before Christmas waiting for that hat to come in the mail. When it finally arrived, I couldn't wait for a day off to wear it. I certainly wasn't going to wear it for work where it would become sweat-stained, dusty, and dirty.

I've used that hat for the last ten years as a go-to-town hat, being careful to not let it get too dirty. I liked it so well that I had another one made in a brown color to match my suit.

Over the years, I've had quite a few compliments on the hat. Strangers would walk up to me and say, "That sure is a good looking hat you've got," or "Nice looking hat!"

A mere "thank you" didn't seem like quite enough, so I started telling folks—and it's the truth—"I've had a lot of compliments on this hat, but I haven't had many on the head underneath it!"

Training

All of our help has to go through a training session at the beginning of the season. This training session consists mostly of reviewing safety procedures around the horses and dudes. The dudes, or tourists, are generally out of their element around the horses and a review of safety procedures is quite necessary to keep everyone on their toes, particularly with the more inexperienced help.

The training sessions are held all summer long, sometimes being held immediately after someone had committed a gross infraction of the rules.

One of the items stressed is that nobody should put a tourist on a horse while the horse is still tied to the rail. This is quite dangerous, as something could spook the horse and the horse could pull back. Most of the time if the horse pulls back, and if the halter or lead rope doesn't break, he'll then jump forward. If he does this with a rider in the saddle and the rider doesn't fall off when the horse pulls back, the rider will generally fall off when the horse jumps forward. If the wrangler is between the rail and the horse when he jumps forward, the wrangler could

get mashed pretty good. This can be a fairly dangerous situation for the tourist and the horse wrangler.

The new hands are also cautioned about bridling and tightening cinchas while a horse is tied to the rail. Sometimes this can cause a horse to pull back, particularly if it's not done right. A bit being forced into a horse's mouth can hurt if it's jammed against his teeth, and the sudden pulling of a cincha around a horse's belly can cause a horse to pull back.

We do have some horses that are habitual "pull backs," and these horses aren't tied to the rail. They'll generally just stand while they're being bridled and the cinchas are tightened.

One horse, a big tall Standardbred named Giraffe, was a notorious pull back. One day, Crystal, one of the hands, was fitting her to a saddle and went to fit a bridle to her and she pulled back. Giraffe wouldn't give in until something broke. When it did, Giraffe flipped over backwards. I was sure glad no one was on her, and I was almost certain the tree of the saddle had been broken. But everything was all right, even Giraffe.

Dave, the boss, had witnessed the whole affair and he went to bridle Giraffe. He had some trouble because the horse kept holding her head up and backing up to boot!

When he finally got the job done, he told everyone, "This horse is a pull back. Don't ever tie her to the rail. And get either Stu or myself to bridle her!"

I knew that meant that I would be bridling the horse all the time. That was all right with me; I knew enough to untie the horse each time I bridled her. I also found out that she would only back up a few feet when I went to bridle her. But she still held her head high and that made for some difficult work. But as the summer progressed, she did start to lower her head and the bridling got easier. Sometimes the hands wouldn't come and get me to bridle her, and this always made for a difficult time the next time I had to bridle her.

One old horse, Colby, was a notorious pull back. He was just a kid's horse, and he would have been sent to a kid's camp, except for the fact that he was a pull back. He had been Dave's guide horse when he was younger, and, according to Dave, he had bucked off quite a few good hands in the past. He was over that now, and relagated to hauling kids around the trail. Even with his bad habit of pulling back, we kept him around. He was a pensioner, generally only working one two-hour ride a day.

We had hired a young couple from Kentucky that was pretty green in the horse business. Chad could ride some, but he certainly wasn't a bronc rider. Rachel had to be taught everything from the ground up. They had come to work for us because they were mountain climbers.

I found out later that they had originally applied in the Smokey Mountains because they wanted to climb mountains. They hadn't got the jobs there and applied to us because they thought it would be fun to work with the horses. I think the highlight of their summer was when they climbed Longs Peak in Rocky Mountain National Park.

Rachel had some trouble with one horse we called Sunshine. I really liked the horse—she was built real good and looked to me like she had promise. She could have been a halter prospect except for the fact that she had some bumps along her belly. I never thought the horse needed special handling other than she didn't neck rein. When I rode her, I used a snaffle bit and started to teach her some. When we rented her out, I always told the rider about her not neck reining and tried to put more experienced riders on her.

I don't know what happened. When Rachel went to tighten Sunshine's cincha or bridle her, she pulled back and started bucking down the outside of the rail. This caused a lot of horses to pull back, but fortunately their lead ropes and halters held.

We hadn't called any customers out to get on their horses yet, so nobody was hurt. Sunshine had brushed up against Rachel causing her to have some minor abrasions, but she wasn't seriously hurt. I never did find out what set Sunshine off, but another training session was called for.

Because of Rachel's relative inexperience, I never did send her out on a ride by herself. She knew all the trails, having accompanied a lot of rides, but I didn't think she knew enough to handle any situation that might arise. I was careful not to send Chad and Rachel out on the same ride. I thought they might spend too much time watching each other and not enough time watching the tourists.

Chad and I had some heated discussions about Rachel not taking out rides by herself. It got so heated one time that I told Chad, "If you think you can do this job better than me, you can have it!" I was pretty confident in my job security and my abilities. I have always maintained that our customer's welfare came first.

It was a tough summer with the hired help that year, and Chad's protective attitude towards Rachel wasn't making the summer any easier.

I was very surprised when Dave sent Rachel on a four-hour ride by herself. There were only two people, a man and his wife. It was late in the summer and I still didn't have much faith in Rachel's abilities as a trail guide.

After they left, I questioned Dave. "Do you think that's a good idea? She's still pretty green."

"They'll get along okay." Dave knew what I was thinking. He said, "The tourists have horses of their own and they ride a lot where they live. They actually have more horse experience than Rachel. And I told Rachel to make sure she brought them back alive without incident!"

Chad got himself into an embarrassing situation later on that summer. He was going to accompany a ride as an extra guide, and was the last one to leave the stables. He was talking to Dave as he got his horse ready. He got the cincha pulled, got the horse bridled, got on, and prepared to trot off and join the ride. Only he wasn't going anywhere!

Dave was down on one knee having a good laugh. I was standing nearby, watching.

Chad had forgotten to untie his horse! Sheepishly, Chad got off and untied his horse. He didn't say anything as he got back on and walked his horse up to the ride.

"I don't know what good the trainin' does if our hands don't apply it to themselves," I said.

"Just keep training, Stu," said Dave. "You can't do too much training! It's a good thing that Chad's horse isn't a pull back."

Dick Bolton

Dick was about my age, maybe a little older. He'd been a cow-boy most of his life and was a good hand with a horse. I knew Dick from some other functions, and we had a lot in common. Quite often Dick and I would show up at the same affair and find ourselves sitting alone, the more civilized folks staying away from us cowboys. It was all right, Dick and me could talk horses and cattle, which was more interesting to me than what the other folks had to say.

I was surprised when Dick called me one day.

"Do you need any help up there?"

I was always looking for good help. Most of the time I was reduced to hiring college-age kids that hadn't had much experience. The good ranch kids generally had to go back to the ranch and help out during the summer.

"I can always use good help," I answered. I knew Dick always had day work on cow outfits out on the eastern plains of Colorado. I couldn't imagine him without work.

"What's up?" I asked.

"My wife and kids are driving me crazy! I need to get away for a while before I go nuts!"

I thought Dick might get a little bored at my stable.

"You might not like it here, Dick. There ain't no cows to chase, all the rides are just walking, an' I generally don't even move my horse faster than a trot an' only when that's necessary. My hired help is all college-age kids an' they generally drive me up the wall. They don't know as much as they've led me to believe they do. An' the pay ain't much, but I do furnish room an' board. You might not like this."

"But Stu," countered Dick, "you don't understand. My wife and kids are driving me crazy!"

"But how would you get along with my college-age hands?"

"Them kids wouldn't keep tryin' to borrow money from me," Dick interrupted.

"With the wages I pay, you wouldn't be able to lend out any money!"

"That's not important," replied Dick. "The point is that I just need to get away for a while."

"Well, I can use you 'till the middle of September if you'll work for what I pay and don't mind working for a younger man." I had to throw in a little dig at Dick about his age.

"Can I bring my own horse?"

I had been reluctant to allow private horses on the place. My horses already had their own pecking order established, and I didn't want to stand the liability if someone else's horse got hurt. Then, too, I didn't want any of my horses injured by a stranger.

"I've never allowed that before, Dick. I don't want to be responsible if something happens."

"Ol' Babe can handle herself," answered Dick.

"How does she get along with other horses?"

"She won't be a problem," Dick replied.

Dick showed up a couple of days later with his horse trailer and Babe. Babe was a good looking roan mare, probably only seven or eight years old.

Dick saddled Babe and was ready to go to work. He didn't know any of the trails, so I sent him out with Ben, my youngest boy, as an outrider just to learn the trails. Ben and Dick made a pretty good team, leastways it appeared that way. Their riders always came in happy and they seemed to make good tips.

One day, in between rides, Dick was putting Babe through her paces. It's a good idea to keep a horse tuned up when they're doing somewhat of a monotonous job. I imagine the horses get pretty bored walking the same trails everyday. But Dick had captivated Ben's attention, or rather Babe had.

Dick was making Babe back up, spin, and side-pass, seemingly without effort. I was watching from the porch of the office.

"I never knew a horse could do that," said Ben.

"Its pretty simple when you teach them how," said Dick.

"How do you teach them?" asked Ben.

And so began Ben's training as a horse trainer. A lot of the horses that I owned had been ranch horses and could spin, side-pass and back up. I knew this because I'd rode the horses and had put them through their paces. They just needed a little tune-up. There's not much use for these kinds of maneuvers at a dude stable, so the horses weren't used to doing them. With some practice, they would become good at it again.

I mentioned this to Dick.

"I kinda figured that," said Dick. "But I haven't told Ben that. He thinks he's teaching those horses that already know how to do that stuff, but actually the horses are teaching him. He's learning more and quicker this way."

I thought that was a pretty good way to go about it.

A Surprise

Glenna was a good friend. She had cooked for us in hunting camp outside Craig, Colorado. When I was managing the stables in Grand Lake, she used to come up and visit occasionally.

When I got my own stables in Grand County, Colorado, I had a surprise phone call from Glenna. I hadn't heard from her or seen her for a few years. She wanted to know if she could come up and visit for a few days.

"Sure, you can come up," I said. "We can even put you up. We've got plenty of room in the girl's dorm."

"I just need to get to the mountains for a little time." Going to the mountains was Glenna's way of relaxing.

"Can I bring my horses?"

"Sure," I said. "We've got plenty of room. But we can't put your horses up in the girl's dorm. We've got plenty of room in the corrals."

A few days later, she showed up with her horses. She had two Palominos. They were pretty fair looking horses, but I suspected Glenna had bought them mostly because of their color. One was an older mare, pretty well broke, and the other one was a young mare, just green broke.

After some bragging about her horses and telling me all their good points, I gave her a couple of compliments on the horses. I thought she was kinda fishing for compliments in the first place. She seemed real pleased with my comments, and then I put the icing on the cake.

"Are you looking to sell the horses?"

The answer was a very positive, "No!"

Glenna was very pleased with her horses and didn't want to part with them. Generally, that's all it takes to make a good horse—having the owner very pleased with them.

I thought it might be a good idea to send Glenna out on some of our rides. I had her saddle one of her horses and wanted her to accompany my oldest boy, Will, on a large ride.

I was a little surprised when she saddled the younger mare.

"She needs the riding," was Glenna's comment.

Sam, Will's younger brother, was leading the ride. Will was in the middle and Glenna brought up the rear. I watched as Glenna and her young mare fell into line, following the other horses. Glenna's horse seemed to be well mannered and walked right out.

"They won't have any problems," I said to myself as I walked back into the office to answer the phone.

Since we started our business, it had grown to the point where we needed a full-time office person. I had tried to hire such a person, but without success. Will and my other boys didn't like it, and the other people I tried couldn't keep track of the number of horses we'd saddled, the kinds of horses, the number of people we'd scheduled, and the other details of the job. Hence, the job was relegated to me.

It got so bad that one day, while I was finishing up making a reservation, the phone rang. Will answered it. He answered a few questions then said, "Hold on just a minute. I'll let you talk to our reservationist." He handed the phone to me.

R. LOREN SCHMIDT

"Reservationist!" I was dismayed. I owned this company and had been demoted! I got the reservation, and then spent some time contemplating my position in this company. True, I didn't get out and get horseback as often as I'd like to, and true, I generally didn't even saddle a horse in the morning, and true, no one could do this job as good as I could. The stark realization hit me! I was no longer just an old cowboy, I was now a businessman!

Will, Sam, and Glenna returned. Sam led the ride to our dismounting area and Will and Glenna trotted around to the front to tie up their horses and help get the dudes off.

As I left the office to help, I made a move that spooked Blister, Will's horse, some. Blister shied a little, but Will maintained control.

When Blister shied, Glenna's young yeller horse stopped suddenly. This threw Glenna forward in the saddle, and her feet went backward, right into the young mare's flanks.

The young mare bogged her head and started to buck. Glenna only lasted about two jumps, then fell off. She hit the ground pretty hard!

"Your little mare can buck real good," I said as I helped her get up.

"She's never done that before."

"If you want, we can take her the rest of the summer an' ride that out of her."

"No," said Glenna. "I'll just have to do that myself."

Glenna loaded up her horses a few days later. She outdid herself in thanking me for a few days in the mountains. She was also very adamant in thanking me for the big bruise on her hip!

No Sense of Humor

Signing people in for horseback rides can sometimes be a time consuming process. Back in the old days, a person would come in, pay his money, get his horse, be pointed in the right direction, and go for a horseback ride. People were generally unsupervised and what they did was known only to them. When a horse would show up riderless, a wrangler would get a horse, lead the riderless horse out and hunt for the unfortunate soul that had lost his horse.

When a number of costly lawsuits started to emerge, outfitters started having to provide guides and supervised rides. Also, waivers of liability started to appear.

These waivers were generally written by lawyers and consequently became quite long trying to cover every possible mishap. Some prospective riders would insist on reading every word of the waiver, taking all the time they needed. This presented a problem to me, not because there was anything in the waiver I didn't want them to see, but because it would hold up the ride. If one ride left late, we would generally run late the rest of the day.

I felt that if a person was scheduled to leave at one o'clock on a ride, they should leave at one o'clock and not at one-thirty.

In an effort to speed up the sign-in process at my stable, I started to summarize the form for the customers.

"This is a waiver of liability," I would say. "Very basically what it says is, that 'if you fall off, get kicked, stepped on, or otherwise injured, we ain't responsible.'"

Then, trying to add a little humor, I would add, "You're welcome to read this if you want to. You ought to be able to tell we ain't responsible just by lookin' at me!"

This would usually bring a laugh, and most folks would just go ahead and sign it. I thought that comment speeded up our sign-in process and we had a little fun with it.

Some years after I sold my stables, I went to work at Moraine Park Stables. I had worked for Dave, the manager, before and was made barn boss. Part of my job was to sign people in and take money.

My spiel about the waiver had worked well in the past and I began using it again. Dave thought it was quite humorous and I believe he enjoyed a chuckle every time he heard it.

I used it so often, I began to get a little tired of it, even though I enjoyed the laugh it brought from the customers.

Then one day, I changed it.

"You ought to be able to tell we ain't responsible," I was saying, "just by looking at him!"

I pointed at Dave, who was standing behind me in the door. The comment caught Dave by surprise and he had a good laugh along with the customers. I was secretly pleased that it had gone over so well.

I used that line, interchanging Dave and myself, quite often. We really had some fun with it.

Then one day, the supervisor of the park system came for a ride. Part of her job is to evaluate each concessionaire's operation within the park system.

I gave my usual spiel about the waiver, and took her and some others out for a two-hour ride. The ride was uneventful and I thought we would get high marks for our performance.

After the ride, the park supervisor came up to me and said, "That was a very good experience, but you can't say that you're not responsible anymore."

"Why not?" I asked.

"Because you are." Her reply was very curt.

I didn't want to get into an argument with her about the liabilities. I had read our waiver many times, and it stressed the fact that our customers rode at their own risk. I also didn't want to get into a discussion about the dumb things the dudes do, and how, most of the time, when they fall off, it's their own fault. Frequently they aren't following directions.

We did get high marks on our performance. Dave showed me the evaluation later.

"I see she didn't say anything about what she said to me," I said, as we discussed it.

"What did she say to you?" Dave asked.

"She told me I couldn't use my phrase about us not being responsible. You know, I only have fun with that."

"Some of our public servants just don't have a sense of humor."

R. Loren Schmidt—Cowboy,
Artist, and Educator

Loren is still riding despite being afflicted with Parkinson's disease, as evidenced by the photo above, taken during a fund-raising event for Parkinson's disease research. And Loren is still drawing and painting, although he says, "Sometimes my hand gets to shaking so bad, the paint brush flies out of my hand. I get paint where it shouldn't be an' I have to start over!"

In true cowboy fashion, he starts over and finishes what he started.

Loren also teaches an art class in Truth or Consequences, New Mexico.

Other Books by Stu Campbell

Horsing Around a Lot

Horsing Around the Dudes